First World War
and Army of Occupation
War Diary
France, Belgium and Germany

2 CAVALRY DIVISION
Divisional Troops
3 Brigade Ammunition Column
13 October 1914 - 26 February 1918

WO95/1123/5

The Naval & Military Press Ltd
www.nmarchive.com
Published in association with The National Archives

Published by

The Naval & Military Press Ltd

Unit 10 Ridgewood Industrial Park,
Uckfield, East Sussex,
TN22 5QE England
Tel: +44 (0) 1825 749494

www.naval-military-press.com
www.nmarchive.com

This diary has been reprinted in facsimile from the original. Any imperfections are inevitably reproduced and the quality may fall short of modern type and cartographic standards.

© **Crown Copyright**
Images reproduced by permission of The National Archives, London, England, 2015.

Contents

Document type	Place/Title	Date From	Date To
Heading	2nd Cavalry Divisional Artillery. Originally 3rd Brigade R.H.A. Amn. Col. 2nd Cavalry Divisional Ammunition Column R.H.A. 13th October 1914-3rd January 1915. to Feb 1918		
War Diary		13/10/1914	23/11/1914
War Diary		01/12/1914	31/12/1914
War Diary		02/12/1914	14/12/1914
War Diary		01/01/1915	03/01/1915
Heading	Division 2nd Cavalry Ammn Coln Vol II 3-24.1.15		
War Diary		03/01/1915	17/01/1915
War Diary	Petit-Bois-Pihem-Bientques	20/01/1915	24/01/1915
Heading	2nd Cav. Div. Ammn. Col. Vol III 1-27.2.15.		
War Diary	Petit-Bois Vieux-Berquin	01/02/1915	27/02/1915
War Diary	Vieux-Berquin-Grand Bois	27/02/1915	27/02/1915
Heading	2nd Cav. Divl. Ammn. Col. Vol IV. 3-27.3.15.		
War Diary		03/03/1915	09/03/1915
War Diary	Grand-Bois Vieux Berquin	10/03/1915	27/03/1915
Heading	2nd Cavalry Divl. Ammn. Coln. Vol V. 2-30.4.15.		
War Diary		02/04/1915	26/04/1915
War Diary	Reninghelst	27/04/1915	30/04/1915
Heading	2nd Cavalry Division. 2nd Cavy. Divl. Ammn. Col. Vol VI. 1-31.5.15.		
War Diary		01/05/1915	17/05/1915
War Diary	Lagorgue	18/05/1915	31/05/1915
Heading	2nd Cavalry Division. 2nd Cavy. Divl. Ammn. Coln. Vol VII. 1-9.6.15		
War Diary		01/06/1915	09/06/1915
Heading	2nd Cavalry Division. 2nd Cavy. Divl. Ammn. Coln. Vol IX. July 1915.		
War Diary		01/07/1915	20/07/1915
Heading	2nd Cavalry Division. 2nd Cavy. Division Ammn. Coln Vol VIII. From 3-6.8.15.		
War Diary		03/08/1915	12/08/1915
War Diary		06/08/1915	06/08/1915
Heading	2nd Cavalry Division 2nd Cavy. Divl. Ammn. Coln. (3rd Bde R.H.A.) Vol IX. Sept 15.		
Heading	War Diary of the 2nd Cavalry Division Ammn. Column for the Month Sept 1915.		
War Diary		04/09/1915	30/09/1915
Heading	2nd Cavalry Division 3rd Bde R.H.A. Ammn. Coln. Vol X. Oct 15.		
War Diary		03/10/1915	31/10/1915
Heading	2nd Cav. Div. Ammn. Col. Nov 1915. Vol XI.		
War Diary		20/11/1915	30/11/1915
Heading	2nd Cav Div. Ammn. Col. Dec 1915. Vol XII.		
War Diary		01/12/1915	05/12/1915
War Diary		02/12/1915	31/12/1915
Heading	2nd Cav. Ammn. Col. Jan 1916. Vol XIII.		
War Diary		04/01/1916	25/01/1916
War Diary		08/01/1916	31/01/1916

Type	Location	From	To
War Diary		03/02/1916	28/02/1916
War Diary		22/02/1916	22/02/1916
War Diary		02/02/1916	26/02/1916
War Diary	Merck St Lieven. (Pas de Calais)	01/03/1916	31/03/1916
War Diary	Merck St Lieven	06/03/1916	31/03/1916
War Diary		08/04/1916	14/04/1916
War Diary		28/04/1916	28/04/1916
War Diary		01/05/1916	31/05/1916
War Diary		01/05/1916	13/05/1916
War Diary		29/05/1916	29/05/1916
War Diary	Merck-St-Lieven	14/06/1916	18/06/1916
War Diary	Merck St Lieven-Borre	21/06/1916	21/06/1916
War Diary	Borre	23/06/1916	30/06/1916
Heading	War Diary of 2nd Cavalry Divisional Ammunition Column. From: 1st July to 31st July. 1916 (Volume XXIII.)		
War Diary	Borre-Les Cinq Rues (Hazebrouck)	08/07/1916	08/07/1916
War Diary	Les Cinq Rues	15/07/1916	30/07/1916
Heading	War Diary of Ammunition Column 2nd Cav. Div. for August, 1916. Vol 20.		
War Diary	Lescinq Rues-Abeele	06/08/1916	06/08/1916
War Diary	Lescinq Rues.	23/08/1916	23/08/1916
War Diary	Lescinq Rues-Abeele.	25/08/1916	25/08/1916
Heading	War Diary of Ammunition Column, 2nd Cavalry Division for September, 1916. Vol. 21		
War Diary	Lescinq Rues (Hazebrouck)	04/09/1916	04/09/1916
War Diary	Les Cinq Rues.	06/09/1916	06/09/1916
War Diary	Busnes	06/09/1916	07/09/1916
War Diary	Wavrans	07/09/1916	08/09/1916
War Diary	St Georges.	08/09/1916	10/09/1916
War Diary	Remaisnil	10/09/1916	11/09/1916
War Diary	Vignacourt.	11/09/1916	12/09/1916
War Diary	Bonnay	12/09/1916	15/09/1916
Heading	War Diary of 2nd Cavalry Divl. Ammunition Column. October, 1916. Vol 22.		
War Diary	Bonnay	01/10/1916	29/10/1916
Heading	War Diary of 2nd Cavalry Divisional Ammunition Column. November, 1916. Vol. XXVII.		
War Diary	Bonnay	06/11/1916	08/11/1916
War Diary	Bonnay-Bussy	08/11/1916	08/11/1916
War Diary	Bussy-Belloy-Sur-Somme	09/11/1916	09/11/1916
War Diary	Belloy-Sur-Somme-Grand Lavieres	10/11/1916	10/11/1916
War Diary	Grand Lavieres-Ponches Estruval	11/11/1916	11/11/1916
War Diary	Ponches Estruval-Estrees-Les-Crecy	17/11/1916	17/11/1916
War Diary	Estrees-les-Crecy	20/11/1916	20/11/1916
Heading	War Diary of 2nd Cavalry Divisional Ammunition Column. December, 1916. Vol 24.		
War Diary	Estrees-les-Crecy	01/12/1916	31/12/1916
Heading	War Diary of 2nd Cavalry Divisional Ammunition Column. January, 1917. Vol. XXIX.		
War Diary	Estrees-les-Crecy.	09/01/1917	17/01/1917
Heading	War Diary of 2nd Cavalry Divisional Ammunition Column. February, 1917. Vol. XXX.		
War Diary	Estrees-Les-Crecy	04/02/1917	16/02/1917
Heading	War Diary of 2nd Cavalry Divisional Ammunition Column. March, 1917. Vol. XXXI.		

War Diary	Estrees-Les-Crecy	01/03/1917	23/03/1917
Heading	War Diary of 2nd Cavalry Divisional Ammunition Column. April, 1917. Vol. XXXII.		
War Diary	Estrees Les Crecy Bealcorut	05/04/1917	05/04/1917
War Diary	Bealcourt Henu	08/04/1917	08/04/1917
War Diary	Henu	09/04/1917	30/04/1917
Heading	War Diary of 2nd Cav. Divl. Ammunition Column. R.H.A. May, 1917-Vol. XXXIII.		
War Diary	Henu-Naours.	12/05/1917	12/05/1917
War Diary	Naours-Aubigny	13/05/1917	13/05/1917
War Diary	Aubigny	13/05/1917	13/05/1917
War Diary	Aubigny-Lamotte	14/05/1917	14/05/1917
War Diary	Aubigny	14/05/1917	14/05/1917
War Diary	Lamotte-Marquaix	15/05/1917	15/05/1917
War Diary	Marquaix	16/05/1917	31/05/1917
Heading	War Diary of 2nd Cavalry Division Ammunition Column from 1st June to 30th June 1917. Volume XXXIV.		
War Diary	Marquaix	02/06/1917	14/06/1917
War Diary	Marquaix	01/06/1917	30/06/1917
Heading	War Diary of Ammunition Column R.H.A. 2nd Cavalry Division from 1st to 31st July 1917. Volume No. XXXV.		
War Diary	Marquaix	07/07/1917	11/07/1917
War Diary	Marquaix-Suzanne	13/07/1917	13/07/1917
War Diary	Suzanne-Ville Sur. Corbie.	14/07/1917	14/07/1917
War Diary	Ville Sur Corbie-Sarton	15/07/1917	15/07/1917
War Diary	Sarton-Locheux	16/07/1917	16/07/1917
War Diary	Lucheux-La Thieloye	27/07/1917	27/07/1917
War Diary	Lucheux	27/07/1917	27/07/1917
War Diary	La Thieloye-Olhain	28/07/1917	28/07/1917
War Diary	Olhain-Sailly-Laboruse	29/07/1917	29/07/1917
War Diary	Lucheux-Berlencourt	29/07/1917	29/07/1917
War Diary	Sailly-Labourse	31/07/1917	31/07/1917
War Diary	War Diary of the Ammunition Column R.H.A. 2nd Cavalry Division from 1.8.17 to 31.8.17. Volume XXXVII		
War Diary	Sailly Labourse.	01/08/1917	19/08/1917
War Diary	Berlencourt	02/08/1917	09/08/1917
War Diary	Sailly Labourse-Olhain	19/08/1917	19/08/1917
War Diary	Olhain-Berlencourt	20/08/1917	20/08/1917
War Diary	Berlencourt	31/08/1917	31/08/1917
Heading	War Diary of Ammunition Column RHA 2nd Cavalry Division from Sept 1st to 30th 1917. Volume XXXVII.		
War Diary	Berlencourt-Bajus	05/09/1917	05/09/1917
War Diary	Bajus-Hesdinguel	06/09/1917	06/09/1917
War Diary	Hesdinguel-Fosse No.2 (2000 yds. W of Les Brebis)	08/09/1917	08/09/1917
War Diary	Fosse No 2-Verquinel	15/09/1917	15/09/1917
War Diary	Flers.	16/09/1917	16/09/1917
War Diary	Verquinel-Bethune	21/09/1917	21/09/1917
War Diary	Bethune	25/09/1917	25/09/1917
War Diary	Flers.	25/09/1917	25/09/1917
War Diary	Bethune	30/09/1917	30/09/1917
Heading	War Diary of the Ammunition Column R.H.A. 2nd Cavalry Division from 1st October to 31st October 1917. Volume XXXVIII.		

War Diary	Flers-Lathieuloye	01/10/1917	08/10/1917
War Diary	Bethune-La Thieuloye	09/10/1917	09/10/1917
War Diary	La Thieuloye	12/10/1917	12/10/1917
War Diary	La Thieuloye-Etree Wamin	20/10/1917	20/10/1917
War Diary	Etree-Wamin-St Leger Domart	21/10/1917	21/10/1917
War Diary	St Leger Les Domart-Plachy-Buyon	22/10/1917	22/10/1917
War Diary	Plachy-Buyon	31/10/1917	31/10/1917
Heading	War Diary of Ammunition Column RHA 2nd Cavalry Division from 1st to 30th November 1917. Volume I.		
War Diary	Plachy-Buyon.-Proyart	16/11/1917	16/11/1917
War Diary	Proyart-Montecourt	17/11/1917	17/11/1917
War Diary	Montecourt-Villers-Faucon	21/11/1917	21/11/1917
War Diary	Villers-Faucon-Villers-Pluich	21/11/1917	22/11/1917
War Diary	Villers-Faucon.	23/11/1917	30/11/1917
Heading	War Diary of the Ammunition Column RHA 2nd Cavalry Division from 1st to 31st December 1917. Volume XL		
War Diary	Villers-Faucon-Fins	01/12/1917	01/12/1917
War Diary	Fins-Etricourt.	02/12/1917	02/12/1917
War Diary	Etricourt.	02/12/1917	02/12/1917
War Diary	Etricourt-Metz	06/12/1917	06/12/1917
War Diary	Etricourt-Susanne	06/12/1917	06/12/1917
War Diary	Suzanne-Vers.	07/12/1917	07/12/1917
War Diary	Metz-Bouly.	08/12/1917	08/12/1917
War Diary	Boucly.	12/12/1917	31/12/1917
War Diary	Vers	31/12/1917	31/12/1917
Heading	War Diary of Ammunition Column 3rd Brigade R.H.A. 1st January 1918 to 31st January 1918. Volume XLI		
War Diary	Boucly	08/01/1918	08/01/1918
War Diary	Caulaincourt	24/01/1918	24/01/1918
Heading	War Diary of Ammunition Column 3rd Brigade R.H.A. From February 1st to 28th 1918 Volume XLIII		
War Diary	Caulaincourt	01/02/1918	28/02/1918
War Diary	Caulaincourt	12/02/1918	26/02/1918

2nd Cavalry Divisional Artillery.

Originally 3rd~~Cavalry~~ Brigade R.H.A. Amn.Col.

2nd CAVALRY DIVISIONAL AMMUNITION COLUMN R.H.A.

13th OCTOBER 1914 - 3rd JANUARY 1915.

to
Feb. 1918

Army Form C. 2118.

WAR DIARY
or
INTELLIGENCE SUMMARY.
(Erase heading not required.)

Hour, Date, Place	Summary of Events and Information	Remarks and references to Appendices
13-10-14	To CAËSTRE	G.S. wagons are hopeless things on narrow and bad roads and misplaced arm arrangements comrd[?].
14 -		
15 -	To GYANT CAPPELS	
16-10-14 (Friday)	Joined 2ⁿᵈ CAV. DIV. AMN. COLUMN. To WYTCHAETE 3 & 4 each 2 AM each.	
20-10-14	To KEMMEL. Joined & released section 4 GROOTVERSTAAT	
21-10-14 (Wednesday)	To LA CLYTTE. Pickd up ad[vance]d sectn 4 13 Pr & all 3 Batteries each day. Heavy expenditure 13 remount joined	DIV AMN COLUMN to fully 16 keep down up.
27-10-14		The keeping out of an advanced sectn composed entirely of limber wagons is an unmitigated [?] dirty nuisance[?]. Given the difficulty.
1-11-14	To RENINGHELST	
2-11-14	To farm 1 mile N of FONTAINE HOUCK. Established an advanced sectn at front.	An Xtra section would be to have a whole sectn with each CAV BDE (attached to BDE) as is done in 1ˢᵗ CAV. DIV.
12-11-14	2 wtn S of NEUVE EGLISE. This section initialed & moved in every night (as was done by the BRUNT VERSTAAT section). To remain out by day and right. The DIV. AMN. COLUMN (formed by joining the 3ʳᵈ Bde N.W. a Run fd to Hq of BDE Ran fd)	

Army Form C. 2118.

WAR DIARY
or
INTELLIGENCE SUMMARY.
(Erase heading not required.)

Hour, Date, Place	Summary of Events and Information	Remarks and references to Appendices

is now added to it. The attachment of 2 S.A.A.* carts of G.S. wagons from each Regiment is 18 wagons in all. The column 1 km has a strength of about 350 men and 40 horses, and takes about 1200 yds in column of route. [This in spite of the fact that 3 Batteries, column is short of 63 wagons, and 16 G.S. Batts Col. of 16 wagons — therefore the transport together of the two columns at full strength would have produced a much longer column of route] 830 horses and taking about 1 absolutely necessary to keep the Column made its way back, and even after an immense return to supply all 3 Cav. Bdes; absented return in a useful action with each Bde.

The Column in its arranged condition (i.e. short of 19 wagons G.S. if it was strong as a column for 3 Cav. Bdes) only had about 150 rounds per gun for the 18

*The Cav. Bread ellar is not a good pattern for service. When harness gets wet, and clothing is wearer, it is liable to crumble and cause galls.

The unshifted R.A. pattern is much better.

Army Form C. 2118.

WAR DIARY
or
INTELLIGENCE SUMMARY.
(Erase heading not required.)

Instructions regarding War Diaries and Intelligence Summaries are contained in F.S. Regs., Part II. and the Staff Manual respectively. Title pages will be prepared in manuscript.

Hour, Date, Place	Summary of Events and Information	Remarks and references to Appendices
11-2-14 [11-11-14?]	Guns of the 3 Batteries in 1st Division.* Between 21/10/14 and 1/11/14, the expenditure of 13 Prs has reached at times 1000 rounds per Battery (or 170 rounds per gun) per day. However the Batteries were never short, and though the columns were nearly empty at times, it was always filled again in good time by the Park.	*noted 1/220. as per war Establishments.
14-11-14	Moved to BLEU. Advanced action still remaining out.	
17-11-14	Moved to S¹ YANS CAPPEL and then sent back to VIEUX BERQUIN. — Battalion started to 5ᵗʰ DIV ARTY.	
18-11-14	Advanced action until ..... 15 ...... 1 mile S W ? DRANOUTRE. to supply battains in their new position.	

Army Form C. 2118.

WAR DIARY
or
INTELLIGENCE SUMMARY.
(Erase heading not required.)

Instructions regarding War Diaries and Intelligence Summaries are contained in F. S. Regs., Part II. and the Staff Manual respectively. Title pages will be prepared in manuscript.

Hour, Date, Place	Summary of Events and Information	Remarks and references to Appendices
19 - 11 - 14	S. A. A. cart sent out to get advanced units. Commenced a Cavalry Brigade going up into firing line again	
22. 11 - 14	Relieved and came into reserve. Released orders repaired	
23 - 11 - 14	Household R H A Cav. Column (Just taken out so was 4.5 hours) joined in the Column	
2. 16 31 - 12 - 14	Cavalry Corps in Reserve – Am. Colʼ at VIEUX BERQUIN.	
2 - 12 - 14.	Inspected by H.M. King George V	
9 - 12 - 14	Inspection by F.M. Sir J. French Commanding in Chief.	

Army Form C. 2118.

WAR DIARY
or
INTELLIGENCE SUMMARY.
(Erase heading not required.)

Instructions regarding War Diaries and Intelligence Summaries are contained in F.S. Regs., Part II. and the Staff Manual respectively. Title pages will be prepared in manuscript.

Hour, Date, Place	Summary of Events and Information	Remarks and references to Appendices
14-12-14	Ordered by Cavalry Corps to bring number of Rounds per gun up to 220, an issue down in most Table. The interior an increase of 5 GS wagons, 67 horses + 50 men. At the same time Authority was obtained to exchange 2 G.S. + R Damchosim Am: Cols: for 4 Limbered wagons, so as to form an advanced section when required. This then too shows an establt: the staff 2 the G.O. Am: Col: will be 75 horses with over 500 horses and 400 men in company near by 3/4 Col: 9 words - a 60 Ry cavalry unit. 2/Lt Turner, Garnishaw, Stewart promoted from the ranks. Capt. N.A.L. DAY posted to I Battery RHA	
14-12-14 1-1-15	Maj. W.J. PARSONS posted to New Army - Lt. T.G. DU BUISSON	
3-1-15	Maj. W.J. PARSONS posted from 116 Battery RFA.	

121/4327

Diaries
2nd Cavalry Division ^ "A" Col"

Vol II. 3 — 24.1.15

Army Form C. 2118.

WAR DIARY
or
INTELLIGENCE SUMMARY.
(Erase heading not required.)

Instructions regarding War Diaries and Intelligence Summaries are contained in F.S. Regs., Part II. and the Staff Manual respectively. Title pages will be prepared in manuscript.

Hour, Date, Place	Summary of Events and Information	Remarks and references to Appendices
3-1-15	41 men & 67 horses joined, to complete new establishment.	
10-1-15	Orders received that - full complement of S.A.A to be carried on Am-Cols - & further 12 G.S. wagons assigned to them - on the arrival of these whole, the attached G.S. limbered wagons of Cavalry regiment are to be returned to their own regiment.	
17-1-15 PETIT-BOIS + PIHEM - BIENTQUES	Marched 7.30 a.m. to new billeting area SW of ST OMER. R.Q. went into billet.	
20-1-15	Horses put in under cover in above area	
24-1-15	7 G.S. wagons & 2 limbers G.S. wagons attached with full complement of men and horses	

M S Solomon
Capt R.H.A.
Cdg. Am. Col.
2nd Cav. Div.

121/4464

2nd Cav. Divl: Annl: Coln

Vol XX III 1-27.2.15

Army Form C. 2118.

WAR DIARY
or
INTELLIGENCE SUMMARY.
(Erase heading not required.)

Instructions regarding War Diaries and Intelligence Summaries are contained in F. S. Regs., Part II. and the Staff Manual respectively. Title pages will be prepared in manuscript.

Hour, Date, Place	Summary of Events and Information	Remarks and references to Appendices
1-2-15 7.30am PETIT-BOIS 3pm VIEUX-BERQUIN	Ammunition column marched back to near old billets area at VIEUX BERQUIN	
3-2-15	The 2 G.S. limbered wagons* per cavalry regiment which had been attached to H. Am. Col.ⁿˢ were returned to their own units. 5mm G.S. wagons, 30 L.D., 15-O.R. joined, thus making H. Am. Col.ⁿˢ complete in accordance with War Establishment	* The limber hooks of the G.S. limbered wagons are too weak and on constantly breaking. This means that the hind part frequently together to be left behind as half the load is lost.
5-2-15		
6-2-15	2/Lt. G.L.A. Duff joined from 124ᵗʰ Battery R.F.A. on posting to 28ᵗʰ Battery R.F.A. on posting to E.J. Battery R.H.A.	
7-2-15	Capt.ⁿ C.G. LAWSON & K. PARBURY left on posting to 28ᵗʰ Battery R.F.A. on posting E.J. Battery R.H.A. 2 LT. T.G. DU BUISSON left on posting E.J. Battery R.H.A.	
8-2-15	The Amⁿ Colⁿ was reorganised into two echelons, a light and heavy, vide A.D. App. I. There was no alteration from the authorised War Establishment. The two echelons will	

Army Form C. 2118.

WAR DIARY
or
INTELLIGENCE SUMMARY.
(Erase heading not required.)

Instructions regarding War Diaries and Intelligence Summaries are contained in F. S. Regs., Part II. and the Staff Manual respectively. Title pages will be prepared in manuscript.

Hour, Date, Place	Summary of Events and Information	Remarks and references to Appendices
14-2-15	It was settled when working, but when any fighting is going on, the light echelon will be pushed forward than the heavy, and batteries & brigade will be supplied with ammunition from the light echelon, which in turn will be refilled from the heavy echelon & from the Am. Park when possible. See App. I.	A motor cyclist was sent to the Am. Col. by the Am. Park when fighting. He was found inadequate. Recommends that a wireless section be permanently attached to Am. Column.
19-2-15	On two-wheel G.S. wagon the carriage of explosives to be added to the Establishment, and attached to the Heavy Echelon, under authority of P. & G.	
27-2-15 8 a.m. VIEUX-BERQUIN — 3.30 p.m. GRAND BOIS	2/Lt. T. R. ANDERSON joined on posting from Secunderabad. (as Bde. Am. Col.) Marches followed via HAZEBROUCK & EBLINGHEM to GRAND BOIS — PIHEM — BLENTQUES.	

W. J. Downer
Capt. R.H.A.

2nd Cav: Div: Annex "C"
Vol IV — 3 — 27.5.15

Army Form C. 2118.

WAR DIARY
or
INTELLIGENCE SUMMARY.
(Erase heading not required.)

Hour, Date, Place	Summary of Events and Information	Remarks and references to Appendices
3-3-15	2/Lr H.B. RUSSELL RFA and 2/Lr A.B. THORNE RFA S.R. joined "attached for duty". Am⁰ Col⁰ for Cav. Div. N⁰ 3 (Cav Bde. in future to consist of HdQrs & 3 Sections as in War Establishment. These involve the loss of 1 Captain, 1 R.S.M., 1 R.Q.M.S., 1 Far. Sgt., 1 Cpl. S.S., 1 Bomb., and a few gunners, drivers, and horses. ※	※ See App II. When organised to heavy Hyd-echelon now the need of a second R.S.M., R.Q.M.S., Far Sgt., S.S. is keenly felt.
9-3-15 6am GRAND-BOIS 3pm VIEUX BERQUIN	Marched from WITTES & STEENBECQUE to old billeting area near VIEUX BERQUIN	
10 - 13/3-15	Standing to all day	
13-3-15	A detachment of Brigade Am⁰ Col⁰ and Divisional Am⁰ Col⁰ 2 North Midland Territorial division joined - viz⁰/k 2 officers, 84 other ranks, 85 horses, 12 G.S. wagons + 7 G.S. limbered wagons.	

Army Form C. 2118.

WAR DIARY
or
INTELLIGENCE SUMMARY.
(Erase heading not required.)

Instructions regarding War Diaries and Intelligence Summaries are contained in F. S. Regs., Part II. and the Staff Manual respectively. Title pages will be prepared in manuscript.

Hour, Date, Place	Summary of Events and Information	Remarks and references to Appendices
21 March 1915	2" Lt C.L.A. Duff RHA left Lt Chenev & adm Orderly Officer 6/1 Col G. Gillson RHA	
26th March	Captain Hon A.H Stanley joined as Captain M.O learner King fills L.S Battery R.H.A	
27th March	2" Lt R.A. Beck RFA joined attached for duty	

A H Stanley
........................CAPT. R.H.A.
COMMDG. 2nd CAV. DV. AMN. COL

2nd Cavalry Divl Ammn Coln

Vol V   2 — 30.4.15

Army Form C. 2118.

WAR DIARY
or
INTELLIGENCE SUMMARY.
(Erase heading not required.)

Instructions regarding War Diaries and Intelligence Summaries are contained in F. S. Regs., Part II. and the Staff Manual respectively. Title pages will be prepared in manuscript.

Hour, Date, Place	Summary of Events and Information	Remarks and references to Appendices
2nd April	Return N. Midland D.A.C. left to report to rest of the unit.	
6th April	Captain E.R.T. Croxall and 2nd Lt G.M. Dixon joined Warwickshire R.H.A. Amn Column	
7th April	Lt. Hon R.E. Eden joined Warwickshire Battery	
14th April	Warwickshire Battery and its Amn Column ordered to join 9th Canadian Brigade owing to an outbreak of measles or did not start	
17th April	2nd Lt G.M. Dixon posted to Warwickshire Battery	
23rd April	Light Echelon ordered to Estaires ESTAIRES as to Backing was to go into action in LA ?... area. Order cancelled moved instead to FLETRE	
25th April	Light Echelon moved to BOESCHEPE	
26th April	Heavy Echelon marched to BOESCHEPE. Light Echelon to RENINGHELST. Ammunition issued 341 Rounds L.D., 285 L.E., 272 L.T., 76 L. Anti aircraft action	

Army Form C. 2118.

WAR DIARY
or
INTELLIGENCE SUMMARY.
(Erase heading not required.)

Instructions regarding War Diaries and Intelligence Summaries are contained in F.S. Regs., Part II. and the Staff Manual respectively. Title pages will be prepared in manuscript.

Hour, Date, Place	Summary of Events and Information	Remarks and references to Appendices
27th April Reninghelst	393 Rounds issued 96 to "D", 145 to "E", 152 to "J"	
28th April	Heavy Echelon reported Light Echelon at RENINGHEAST "E" 1000 rounds issued 454 rounds to "D", 304 to "E", 204 to "J", 28 to Anti Aircraft Section	
29th April	J Battery 120 rounds	
30th April	D Battery 10/6, 152 rounds, E Battery 228, J Battery 228 rounds	D. Hanley Captain R.H.A. Comdg, "C" C.D. A.C.

2nd Cavalry Division

2nd Cav. Div. Ammn Col.

Vol VII 1 — 31.5.15

12/553³

Army Form C. 2118.

WAR DIARY
or
INTELLIGENCE SUMMARY.
(Erase heading not required.)

Instructions regarding War Diaries and Intelligence Summaries are contained in F.S. Regs., Part II. and the Staff Manual respectively. Title pages will be prepared in manuscript.

Hour, Date, Place	Summary of Events and Information	Remarks and references to Appendices
1st May	200 Rounds issued to No 9 Anti Aircraft Section	
2nd May	Amm Column two R.A. Amn moved at 7.30 p.m to	
	LA SARTHE near MERVILLE.	
4th May	R.A.A left at ZEVECOTEN	
	Lt Anderson ordered to join D" Battery temporarily	
	in place of Dr Waldron wounded.	
5th May	Amm Column marched from LA SARTHE to LA GORGUE	
	and issued the following Amn. 76 L.E, 46 L.J, 416 L.D. Total 185	
6th May	Issued 28 Rounds L.J 55 L.D. Total 83	
7th May	Issued 458 rounds to each of the 3 Batteries. Total 1368	
8 May	Issued 70 Rounds L.E. Total 70	
9th May	Issued 76 Rounds L.E & 176 L.D also 224 L to 18 Anti Aircraft. Total 376	
10th May	Issued 76 L.E. 246 L.J 3 58 L.D Section. Total 380	
11th May	Issued 152 Rounds to E 150 L.J 82 L.D	
14th May	228 " E 111 L.J 121 L.D Total 364	
15th	152 L E 152 L.J 162 L.D Total 460	
16 May	" 316 L.J 29 L.D Total 458	
17	to 18 Anti Aircraft Section 200 rounds 60	
	200	

Army Form C. 2118.

WAR DIARY
or
INTELLIGENCE SUMMARY.
(Erase heading not required.)

Instructions regarding War Diaries and Intelligence Summaries are contained in F.S. Regs., Part II. and the Staff Manual respectively. Title pages will be prepared in manuscript.

Hour, Date, Place	Summary of Events and Information	Remarks and references to Appendices
LAGORGUE		
18.5.15	Issued 240 Rounds 6 E R Hb	
19. 5.15	" 42 " 6 T RHA	
20 5.15	" 38 " G E	
25. 5.15	" 264 " No 18 Amm Subsupply Kolan	
26. 5.15	" 58 " G Battries	
31. 5	marched at 8 pm to Rouescure and joined the S.A. section which had been detached on 4 May. S.A section returned to Vieux Berquin on 3rd and at 5 am 14 th. marched to Ruinghelst where it stayed till 29 th May. On this day it marched to Vieux Berquin on 31.15 to Rouescure.

O. Hanley
CAPT. R.H.A.
COMMDG. 2nd CAV. DIV. AMN. COLUMN

151/5885

2nd Cavalry Division.

2nd Cav: Div: Ammn Coln

Vol VII 1 — 9.6.15.

WAR DIARY of the 2nd Can: Div: A.C.

or

INTELLIGENCE SUMMARY.

(Erase heading not required.)

Army Form C. 2118.

Instructions regarding War Diaries and Intelligence Summaries are contained in F.S. Regs., Part II. and the Staff Manual respectively. Title pages will be prepared in manuscript.

Hour, Date, Place	Summary of Events and Information	Remarks and references to Appendices
1.6.15	Lt T.P. Pearson & 2nd Lt H.J. Trimmer joined & Chasseur to duty.	
9.6.15	2nd Lt H.B. Russell posted to R.F.C. for duty.	

M Stanley
Captain

181/6210

2nd Cavalry Division.

2nd Cav: Div: Amm" Col"

Vol IX May 1915.

a2
a96

WAR DIARY of the 2nd Cav. Div. A.S.

Army Form C. 2118.

INTELLIGENCE SUMMARY

(Erase heading not required.)

Hour, Date, Place	Summary of Events and Information	Remarks and references to Appendices
1.7.15	Establishment increased by 2 chains & 4 horses and 2 Limbered G.S. wagons to furnish 2,000 rounds S.A.A. to late machine gun Battery.	
20.7.15	Moved to Clairmarais	

[signature]

121/6567

ar
a56

2nd Cavalry Division

2nd Cavalry Division Amm" Col"

Col Vett

from 3 - 6. 8. 15

WAR DIARY or INTELLIGENCE SUMMARY.

Army Form C. 2118.

2nd Cavalry Division Ammunition Column August 1915.

Hour, Date, Place	Summary of Events and Information	Remarks and references to Appendices
3/8/15	2nd Lt. L. H. Yielden joined from base.	
5/8/15	Capt. Hon. O. H. Harley posted to 5-2" Bty RHA	
7/8/15	Lt. J. B. Perea assumed command	
7/8/15	Lt. R. B. Thorne attached temporary to W.3L	
12/8/15	Send Mule. Battery.	
	Lt. S. E. Turner joined from base	
	Lt. R.H. Peck posted to Chargenters	
6/8/15	No. column moved to billets at Esquer	

J. B. Perea. L.

121/7052

2nd Cavalry Division

2nd Cavy. Divl: Ammn Coln (3rd Bde RHA.)

Col ₣
Sept. 15.

War Diary of the
2nd Canadian Army Column
to the monotony September 1915

Army Form C. 2118.

WAR DIARY
or
INTELLIGENCE SUMMARY.
(Erase heading not required.)

Hour, Date, Place	Summary of Events and Information	Remarks and references to Appendices
4/9/15	3rd R.H.A Brigade moved towards Pottune. J Battery coming into action Eytt-Edelen & infantry & filled at Querrig. Heavy shelter at Vordn by Pottune.	
6/9/15	2 Gunner	
7/9/15	Suffield D battery 6.5mm of shrapnel	
8/9/15	Suffield J battery with 7.7 mm of shrapnel. D battery with 6.1do shrapnel. D battery 5.2 2do shrapnel Eytt Edelen under shell fire no casualties	
12/9/15	J battery 3.1do shrapnel E battery 34 2do shrapnel	
14/9/15		
15/9/15	E battery 6.5-2do shrapnel D battery 5.9 2do shrapnel	

Army Form C. 2118.

WAR DIARY
or
INTELLIGENCE SUMMARY.
(Erase heading not required.)

Instructions regarding War Diaries and Intelligence Summaries are contained in F. S. Regs., Part II. and the Staff Manual respectively. Title pages will be prepared in manuscript.

Hour, Date, Place	Summary of Events and Information	Remarks and references to Appendices
17/9/15	Returned to Esquires	
21/9/15	Left Esquires and XI to Mametz. Heavy hostile to Esquires.	
24/9/15	Marched 5.30 pm to Mardy Bayeau	
25/9/15	Left Esquires marched 3.30 p -	
28/9/15	Heavy shelling marched to Martry.	
29/9/15	Heavy shells to return Blanche by shells	
30/9/15	To Hoffnay Station to Inspire le Mans. Heavy shells.	

J. Blennie

121/7429

3rd Cavalry Division

3rd Bde. RHA Amm" Col"

Vol X

Oct 15

WAR DIARY

4th Div Am: Col. R.F.A.

INTELLIGENCE SUMMARY.

(Erase heading not required.)

Army Form C. 2118.

Hour, Date, Place	Summary of Events and Information	Remarks and references to Appendices
3.10.15	Light Echelon moved to NORRENT FONTES	
5.10.15	Heavy Echelon moved to ERNY ST JULIEN	
17.10.15	H.E " " L.A SABLONNIÈRE	
	L.E " " LE RONS	
19.10.15	Both Echelons marched to MERCK ST LIEVEN	
27.10.15	Lt N.G. Perry R.F.A. } joined from Base	
	Lt R. Cochrane R.F.A. } attached for duty	
28.10.15	Lt P.Q. Muirhead R.F.A. joined from Base & attached for duty	
29.10.15	Lt C.H. Verden R.F.A. left for England	
31.10.15	Lt A.B. Thorne R.F.A. rejoined from 36th Trench Mortar Battery	

R.F. Trim? Lt. R.F.A.

2nd Cav. D. Ammn. Col.

Nov. 1915.

Vol XI

144/121

Army Form C. 2118.

WAR DIARY
or
INTELLIGENCE SUMMARY.

2nd Cavalry Divison Ammunition Column

(Erase heading not required.)

Hour, Date, Place	Summary of Events and Information	Remarks and references to Appendices
26.10.15	R.F.A. Capt. T.B. PERSSE, struck off the strength sick in England. 2nd Lieut. H.F. TRIM, R.F.A. assumed command.	
27.11.15	2nd Lieut. R.W.H. WILKES, R.F.A. joined and attached for duty.	
29.11.15	13 pr Sections moved with the 3rd Bde R.H.A. One Section (13 pr) was detached with "E" Battery billetted at ECQUES. Two Sections (13 pr) moved to HERBELLES attached to "D" & "J" batteries.	
30.11.15	"D" & "J" Sections moved to LOCON. "E" Battery Section moved to HINGES.	

H.F. Trim 2/Lt R.F.A.

2nd Cav: Dr. Annes. Col.

Dec 1915.
Vol XVI

121/7957

Army Form C. 2118.

WAR DIARY
2nd Cavalry Division Ammunition Column
INTELLIGENCE SUMMARY.

(Erase heading not required.)

Instructions regarding War Diaries and Intelligence Summaries are contained in F.S. Regs., Part II. and the Staff Manual respectively. Title pages will be prepared in manuscript.

Hour, Date, Place	Summary of Events and Information						Remarks and references to Appendices
1. 12.15 to 4.12.15	D. & J. Btis Sections were attached to 46th Division						
	E. Battery Section was attached to 4th Division						
5. 12.15	D. & J. Sections transferred to 19th Div. & E Section to 12th Division						
	Ammunition was supplied during the month as follows.						
		To D Battery		To J Battery		To E Battery	
	High Explosive	Shrapnel	High Explosive	Shrapnel	High Explosive	Shrapnel	
2. 12.15						43 rd	
3. 12.15							
4. 12.15		76 rd				131 rd	
5. 12.15		54 rd					
6. 12.15				58 rd			
7. 12.15		96 rd			1 rd	123 rd	
8. 12.15		64 rd	3 rds	76 rd			
9. 12.15		60 rd				144 rd	
10. 12.15		76 rd		91 rd			
11. 12.15		31 rd		82 rd		152 rd	
12. 12.15		114 rd		90 rd		205 rd	

R.F.Train Capt.RFA

Army Form C. 2118.

WAR DIARY
or
INTELLIGENCE SUMMARY.

(Erase heading not required.)

2nd Cavalry Division Ammunition Column

Instructions regarding War Diaries and Intelligence Summaries are contained in F.S. Regs., Part II. and the Staff Manual respectively. Title pages will be prepared in manuscript.

Summary of Events and Information

Ammunition Supplied —

Hour, Date, Place	To D. Bty.		To J. Bty.		To E. Bty.		Remarks and references to Appendices
	High Explosive	Shrapnel	High Explosive	Shrapnel	High Explosive	Shrapnel	
13. 12. 15		115 rds		152 rds			
14. 12. 15		152 rds		76 rds			
15. 12. 15		152 rds		76 rds	212 rds		
16. 12. 15		—		—	76 rds	4/152 Pr intermediate ra.	
17. 12. 15		76 rds		81 rds		76 rds	
18. 12. 15		152 rds		91 rds		38 rds	
19. 12. 15		152 rds		61 rds		92 rds	
20. 12. 15		—		180 rds		76 rds	
21. 12. 15		—		228 rds			
22. 12. 15		76 rds		118 rds		76 rds	
23. 12. 15		152 rds		—		76 rds	
24. 12. 15		152 rds		300 rds		38 rds	
25. 12. 15		—		—			
26. 12. 15		—		152 rds		138 rds	

R. Irwin Caurkka

Army Form C. 2118.

WAR DIARY
or
INTELLIGENCE SUMMARY.

2nd Canadian Divisional Ammunition Column.
(Erase heading not required.)

Instructions regarding War Diaries and Intelligence Summaries are contained in F.S. Regs., Part II. and the Staff Manual respectively. Title pages will be prepared in manuscript.

Hour, Date, Place	Summary of Events and Information						Remarks and references to Appendices
	Ammunition Supplies:						
	To D. Bty		To J. Bty		To E. Bty		
	High Explosive	Shrapnel	High Explosive	Shrapnel	High Explosive	Shrapnel	
24. 12. 15	-	-	-	76 rds.	-	76 rds.	
28. 12. 15	119	-	-	304 rds.	-	60 rds.	
29. 12. 15	-	-	-	-	-	-	
30. 12. 15	-	-	-	13 rds.	-	-	
31. 12. 15	-	-	-	-	-	-	

M. Main Captn RFA

2nd Cav. Arment. Col.

Jan 1916.
vol XII

Army Form C. 2118.

WAR DIARY
2nd Cavalry Division Ammunition Column
INTELLIGENCE SUMMARY.

(Erase heading not required.)

Instructions regarding War Diaries and Intelligence Summaries are contained in F.S. Regs., Part II. and the Staff Manual respectively. Title pages will be prepared in manuscript.

Hour, Date, Place	Summary of Events and Information	Remarks and references to Appendices
4.1.16	Lieut C.J.L Lutyens joined from "J" Battery. (attached for duty.)	
8 a.m 7-1-16	The Horse 13 pr Section moved to ANNEZIN. The Brigade this day joined the Dismounted Division of Cavalry Corps. Besides supplying the 3rd Cav R.H.A. the Column supplied Grenades, Bombs etc. to the 1st and 3rd Dismounted Brigades.	
9.1.16	2Lieut S.C. TURNER attached to J Battery R.H.A.	
16.1.16	2Lieut N.G. PRING attached for duty from J 13th R.H.A.	
25.1.16	Lieut MARCH from J Battery R.H.A.	
25.1.16	2Lieut C.J.L. LUTYENS posted to 33rd Div.C Arty.	
25.1.16	2Lieut N.G. PRING posted to 23rd Div.C Arty.	

The following ammunition was supplied during the month:-

	"D" Battery		"E" Battery		"J" Battery	
	Shrapnel	High Explosive	Shrapnel	High Explosive	Shrapnel	High Explosive
8.1.16	-	-	-	-	-	-
9.1.16	152 rds	-	152 rds	-	-	-
10.1.16	-	-	-	-	304 rds	-
11.1.16	-	-	304 rds	-	228 rds	-
12.1.16	304 rds	-	-	-	46 rds	-
13.1.16	-	-	-	-	-	-

Army Form C. 2118.

WAR DIARY
INTELLIGENCE SUMMARY.

Ammunition Column H.Q. or 2nd Cavalry Division

Instructions regarding War Diaries and Intelligence Summaries are contained in F. S. Regs., Part II. and the Staff Manual respectively. Title pages will be prepared in manuscript.

(Erase heading not required.)

Hour, Date, Place	"D" Battery R.H.A. Shrapnel	"D" Battery R.H.A. High Explosive	"E" Battery R.H.A. Shrapnel	"E" Battery R.H.A. High Explosive	"J" Battery R.H.A. Shrapnel	"J" Battery R.H.A. High Explosive	Remarks and references to Appendices
14. 1. 16	152 rds	-	152 rds	-	-	-	
15. 1. 16	-	-	-	-	-	-	
16. 1. 16	152 rds	~~rds~~	228 rds	-	160 rds	-	
17. 1. 16	-	-	228 rds	-	-	-	
18. 1. 16	152 rds	-	-	-	-	-	
19. 1. 16	-	-	46 rds	-	-	-	
20. 1. 16	46 rds	-	-	-	46 rds	-	
21. 1. 16	-	-	228 rds	-	-	-	
22. 1. 16	-	-	-	-	-	-	
23. 1. 16	152 rds	-	152 rds	-	46 rds	-	
24. 1. 16	-	-	-	-	-	-	
25. 1. 16	-	-	-	-	-	-	
26. 1. 16	228 rds	-	304 rds	-	30 rds	-	
27. 1. 16	152 rds	-	152 rds	-	-	-	
28. 1. 16	152 rds	-	152 rds	-	152 rds	-	
29. 1. 16	122 rds	30 rds	152 rds	30 rds	152 rds	-	
30. 1. 16							
31. 1. 16					30 rds		

N. T. Irwin Capt. R.F.A.

WAR DIARY or INTELLIGENCE SUMMARY.

(Erase heading not required.)

Army Form C. 2118.

Hour, Date, Place	Summary of Events and Information	Remarks and references to Appendices
3.2.16	Lt. B.O. March R.F.A (SR) attached for duty to "J" Batt. R.H.A.	
4.2.16	2Lt. R.F. Anbas R.F.A (S.R.) joined attached for duty.	
16.2.16	2Lt. A. Cochrane RFA (SR) proceeded to 35th Div: Arty.	
17.2.16	2Lt. W. Wright R.F.A posted joined.	
17.2.16	2Lt. J.W.H. Wilkes RFA (SR) posted.	
18.2.16	2Lt. J.S. Fuller R.F.A attached for duty from HQ 3 7th Bgde R.H.A.	
28.2.16	2Lt. E.W. Austin RFA (S.R.) attached for duty.	
22.2.16	The three 13pr sections marched to MERCK ST LIEVIN and rejoined the 2nd Cavalry Division.	

The following ammunition was expended during the month:—

	"D" Battery		"E" Battery		"J" Battery	
	Shrapnel	H.E.	Shrapnel	H.E.	Shrapnel	H.E.
2.2.16	—	—	76	—	—	—
3.2.16	—	—	152	1	—	—
4.2.16	153	—	152	—	—	—
4.2.16	152	—	—	—	—	—
6.2.16	—	—	159	—	—	—
7.2.16	152	—	—	—	152	—
8.2.16	—	—	152	—	152	—
9.2.16	152	—	152	—	—	—
10.2.16	—	—	152	—	152	—

Army Form C. 2118.

WAR DIARY
or
INTELLIGENCE SUMMARY.
(Erase heading not required.)

Instructions regarding War Diaries and Intelligence Summaries are contained in F.S. Regs., Part II. and the Staff Manual respectively. Title pages will be prepared in manuscript.

Hour, Date, Place	"D" Battery		Summary of Events and Information		"J" Battery		Remarks and references to Appendices
	Shrapnel	H.E	Shrapnel	H.E	Shrapnel	H.E	
11.2.16	76	—	—	—	—	—	
12.2.16	76	—	153	—	—	—	
13.2.16	—	—	152	—	152	—	
14.2.16	76	—	—	—	—	—	
15.2.16	—	—	229	—	380	—	
16.2.16	304	—	304	—	—	—	
17.2.16	—	—	152	—	—	—	
18.2.16	—	—	—	—	—	—	
19.2.16	76	—	—	—	—	—	
20.2.16	—	—	—	—	—	—	
21.2.16	78	—	—	—	82	—	
25.2.16	—	—	154	—	—	—	
26.2.16							

R.J. Trim Capt R.F.A.
Comdg 2nd Cav: Div: Am:Col:

Army Form C. 2118.

WAR DIARY

3rd Brigade Ammunition Column, R.H.A.

INTELLIGENCE SUMMARY.

(Erase heading not required.)

RU/5

Hour, Date, Place	Summary of Events and Information	Remarks and references to Appendices
March 1916. 1st to 31st MERCK St LIEVEN. (Pas. de Calais)	The Column remains in billets at MERCK St LIEVEN, the time being spent in restraining N.C.O.s & men. The horses required particular attention as they had lost condition during the time the Brigade was in action in the previous months.	
MERCK St LIEVEN 6th	2Lieut. J.S. FULLER R.F.A. posted to the 16th Divisional ARTILLERY.	
" 12th	2Lieut. E.W. AUSTIN. R.F.A. (S.R.) posted to R.H.A. Brigade attached 20th Division	
" 26th	2Lieut. S.C. TURNER R.F.A. to "J" Battery R.H.A.	
" 31st	2Lieut. R.F. ANGAS R.F.A. to 32nd Division.	

[signature] Capt. R.F.A.

Army Form C. 2118.

2 Cav Div
Cav Col
Vol 16

WAR DIARY
of
INTELLIGENCE SUMMARY.

(Erase heading not required.)

Instructions regarding War Diaries and Intelligence Summaries are contained in F.S. Regs., Part II. and the Staff Manual respectively. Title pages will be prepared in manuscript.

Hour, Date, Place	Summary of Events and Information	Remarks and references to Appendices
8. 4. 16.	The 3rd Section under 2 Lieut W. WRIGHT took part in an operation scheme with the 3rd Cavalry Brigade.	
14. 4. 16.	2 Lieut W. LUCAS R.F.A. joined from the 2nd Cav: Bri: Ammunition Park.	
28. 4. 16.	2 Lieut W. WRIGHT attached to "E" Battery R.H.A.	
	The Column remained in billets at MERCK ST LIEVEN during the whole month. Its time being occupied in re-training N.C.O. men & getting the horses worked up into good condition. The latter have been much benefited by the rest & attention.	

N. Irvine Capt R.H.A.
FOR CAPT. R.H.A.
COMMDG. 2nd CAV. DIV. AMN. COLUMN, R.H.A.

WAR DIARY of the 3rd Brigade ~~or Army Corps~~ R.H.A.

INTELLIGENCE SUMMARY.

(Erase heading not required.)

Army Form C. 2118.

Hour, Date, Place	Summary of Events and Information	Remarks and references to Appendices
1st to 31st May 1916	Remained in billets at MERCK-St-LIEVEN. Occupied in re-training.	
1st May 1916	LIEUT. A.B. THORNE, RFA. Royal Flying Corps for duty as observer	
"	2/LIEUT. M.N. DEWING, R.F.A. attached for duty from 'E' Battery R.H.A.	
13th May 1916	LIEUT. J.W. AIRD R.F.A. posted from the BASE to duty.	
29th May 1916.	LIEUT. J.W. AIRD and 2/LIEUT M.N. DEWING and 150 other ranks left with horses and digging party and attached to 50th Division	

(signature) .... CAPT. R.F.A.
COMMDG. 2nd CAV. DIV. AMN. COLUMN.

Army Form C. 2118.

WAR DIARY of the 2nd Cavalry Division Am'n Column R.H.A.
INTELLIGENCE SUMMARY.

(Erase heading not required.)

YC 16

Hour, Date, Place	Summary of Events and Information	Remarks and references to Appendices
14.6.16. MERCK-St-LIEVEN	The Light Echelon (3 Officers, 96 other ranks and 142 horses) was detached & proceeded to VLAMERTINGHE to join a Dismounted Brigade formed from the 2nd Cavalry Division.	
17.6.16 MERCK St LIEVEN.	2 Lieut W. WRIGHT R.F.A. joined L'E Battery R.H.A. 2 Lieut M.N DEWING R.F.A. joined.	
6 p.m 18.6.16 MERCK St LIEVEN.	The working party which was dispatched on 29th ult. rejoined.	
3.30 p.m 21.6.16 MERCK St LIEVEN — BORRE	The Heavy Echelon left MERCK St LIEVEN and marched to BORRE arriving at 3 a.m. on the 22nd.	
23.6.16 BORRE	The LIGHT ECHELON rejoined.	
30.6.16 BORRE	2 Lieut R.C. NORTON R.F.A. attached for duty.	

R Mann Capt R.F.A.
CAPT. R.F.A.
COMMDG. 2nd CAV. DIV. AMN. COLUMN

CONFIDENTIAL.

WAR DIARY

of

2nd Cavalry Divisional Ammunition Column.

From: 1st July   to   31st July.1916.

(Volume XXIII.)

Army Form C. 2118.

WAR DIARY of the
2nd Cavalry Division Ammunition Column R.H.A.
INTELLIGENCE SUMMARY.

(Erase heading not required.)

Instructions regarding War Diaries and Intelligence Summaries are contained in F.S. Regs., Part II. and the Staff Manual respectively. Title pages will be prepared in manuscript.

Hour, Date, Place	Summary of Events and Information	Remarks and references to Appendices
2.45 p.m. 8.4.16 BORRÉ - Les cinq Rues (HAZEBROUCK).	In accordance with Orders the Column marched at BORRÉ at 2.45 p.m. arriving at the hamlet of Les cinq Rues (Commune of HAZEBROUCK) at 5 p.m.	
15.7.16. Les cinq Rues.	2 Lieut. C.J.E. ROBINSON, R.F.A. = joined from 2nd DRAGOONS (ROYAL SCOTS GREYS) on promotion to Commissioned rank and temporarily attached to D Battery R.H.A. to instruct in for fortnights instruction.	
24.7.16. Les cinq Rues.	Two detachments of N.C.O's armed under instruction daily in Gun Drill at J.9.E. Batteries R.H.A.	
do.		
30.4.16 Les cinq Rues.	2 Lieut. R.C. NORTON, R.F.A. posted to 33rd Divisional Artillery.	

R. Gmag Capt R.F.A.
Cmag 2nd Cavalry Divisional Amm. Col.
R.H.A.

CONFIDENTIAL.

WAR   DIARY   OF

AMMUNITION   COLUMN
2nd Cav. Div.

for August, 1916.

Army Form C. 2118.

SQ/225

WAR DIARY

2nd Cavalry Division Amm. Column R.H.A.

INTELLIGENCE SUMMARY.

(Erase heading not required.)

Hour, Date, Place	Summary of Events and Information	Remarks and references to Appendices
6.8.16. Leseing Rues. – ABEELE	A working party composed of 100 N.C.Os. & men under the command of 2Lieut W. LUCAS. R.F.A., proceeded to ABEELE near POPERINGHE. Attached to 123rd Field Squadron R.E. to assist in making ammunition stores. Designated "F" Working Party, 2nd Cavalry Division. 2Lieut. C.J.E. ROBINSON, R.F.A. rejoined from "D" Battery R.H.A.	
23.8.16 Leseing Rues.		
25.8.16. Leseing RUES. – ABEELE.	Lieut J.W.H. WILKES relieved 2Lieut W. LUCAS, R.F.A. 4/c of Working Party, the latter rejoining the Column.	

R. Main Capt R.F.A.

SECRET.

WAR DIARY

of

AMMUNITION COLUMN,
2nd CAVALRY DIVISION

for September, 1916.

VOLUME ~~XXV~~

*****

Army Form C. 2118.

WAR DIARY
of the
INTELLIGENCE SUMMARY.
[Erase heading not required.]

2nd Cavalry Div. Ammunition Column R.H.A.

Instructions regarding War Diaries and Intelligence Summaries are contained in F.S. Regs., Part II. and the Staff Manual respectively. Title pages will be prepared in manuscript.

Hour, Date, Place	Summary of Events and Information	Remarks and references to Appendices
4.9.16 Les cing Rues (HAZEBROUCK).	The Working Party rejoined from ABEELE.	
9.30 a.m. 6.9.16 Les cing Rues.	The Division moved S.E. en route to the SOMME. The Ammunition Column left Les cing Rues at 9.30 a.m. and arrived at BUSNES at 3 p.m.	
3 p.m. 6.9.16 BUSNES.		
8.45 a.m. 7.9.16 BUSNES.	Marches at 8.45 a.m. to WAVRANS arriving at 4.30 p.m.	
4.30 p.m. 7.9.16 WAVRANS.		
8.45 a.m. 8.9.16 WAVRANS.	Marched at 8.45 a.m. to St GEORGES near HESDIN arriving at 1.15 p.m.	
1.15 p.m. 8.9.16 St GEORGES.		
9.30 a.m. 10.9.16 St GEORGES.	Marched at 9.30 a.m. to REMAISNIL arriving at 3.50 p.m.	
3.50 p.m. 10.9.16 REMAISNIL.		
7.30 a.m. 11.9.16 REMAISNIL.	Marched at 7.30 a.m. to VIGNACOURT arriving at 1.30 p.m.	
1.30 p.m. 11.9.16 VIGNACOURT.		
10. a.m. 12.9.16 VIGNACOURT.	Marched at 10. a.m. to BONNAY arriving at 6 p.m.	
6 p.m. 12.9.16 BONNAY.		
15.9.16 BONNAY.	The Light Echelon, i.e. the Q.F. wagons and limbered G.S. wagons, was detached, the 13 p.r. wagons being attached to the batteries and the limbered G.S. wagons joining 'A' Echelon of the Cavalry Field Ambulance R.A.M.C. attached to 3rd Brigade R.H.A.	
15.9.16 BONNAY.	Capt C. L. BALKWILL R.A.M.C. attached to 3rd Brigade R.H.A. Head Quarters.	
15.9.16 BONNAY.	2Lieut G. DANIA R.F.A. (S.R.) joined from 34th Div! Art'y. (attached for duty.)	

R.F. Trainer
Capt R.F.A.
Comdg 2nd Can. Div.
A.C.

SECRET.

Vol 22

WAR DIARY

of

2nd CAVALRY DIVL. AMMUNITION COLUMN.

OCTOBER, 1916.

VOL. ~~XXVI.~~

Army Form C. 2118.

WAR DIARY
~~INTELLIGENCE~~ SUMMARY.

(Erase heading not required.)

2nd Cav: Div: Amm" Column.

Instructions regarding War Diaries and Intelligence Summaries are contained in F. S. Regs., Part II. and the Staff Manual respectively. Title pages will be prepared in manuscript.

Hour, Date, Place	Summary of Events and Information	Remarks and references to Appendices
1.10.16 BONNAY.	2Lieut J.W.H. WILKES joins B subsection Light Echelon attached E Battery RHA & was replaced by 2Lieut J.W AIRD, who took charge of the 9 limbered G.S. wagons with A Echelon of the Cavalry.	
10.10.16 BONNAY.	A working party of 1 N.C.O. and 18 men left the Heavy Echelon for duty at H.Q. 3rd Bde R.H.A.	
14.10.16 BONNAY.	A further working party of 10 men joined 3rd Bde R.H.A. H.Q. on Isrigalls group into action.	
19.10.16	Pr. W.T. ELSE was slightly wounded 63049 whilst with the working party but remained at duty.	
29.10.16	Working party rejoined Heavy Echelon on its Brigade coming out of action. Whilst the Brigade was in action the Divisional Amm" Park supplied the Battery wagon lines direct the Heavy Echelon of the Column remaining at BONNAY.	

S.P.Krim Capt. R.F.
COMDG. 2nd CAV. DIV. [illegible]

SECRET.

WAR DIARY

of

2nd CAVALRY DIVISIONAL AMMUNITION COLUMN.

NOVEMBER, 1916.

VOL. XXVII.

Army Form C. 2118.

WAR DIARY

2nd CAVALRY DIVN of the AMMUNITION COLUMN.
INTELLIGENCE SUMMARY.

(Erase heading not required.)

Instructions regarding War Diaries and Intelligence Summaries are contained in F. S. Regs., Part II. and the Staff Manual respectively. Title pages will be prepared in manuscript.

Hour, Date, Place	Summary of Events and Information	Remarks and references to Appendices
6.11.16. BONNAY.	Lieut. J.W.H. WILKES R.F.A. posted for duty to H.Q. 3rd Bde. R.H.A. in relief of 2Lieut. M.N. DEWING.	
8.11.16. BONNAY.	Lieut J. AIRD R.F.A. 99 L.G.S. shot for guns ., S.A.A. Section (attached Cavalry "A" ECHELON) rejoined Heavy Echelon Ammunition Column.	
8.11.16. BONNAY — BUSSY.	Heavy Echelon marched to BUSSY.	
9.11.16. BUSSY — BELLOY-sur-SOMME.	Marched to BELLOY-sur-SOMME.	
10.11.16. BELLOY-sur-SOMME — GRAND LAVIERÉS.	Marched to GRAND LAVIERÉS.	
11.11.16. GRAND LAVIERÉS — PONCHES ESTRUVAL.	Marched to PONCHES ESTRUVAL.	
17.11.16. PONCHES ESTRUVAL — ESTREES-les-CRECY.	Moved to ESTREES-les-CRECY.	
30.11.16. ESTRÉES-les-CRECY	2Lieut. M.N. DEWING relieves 2Lieut W. LUCAS 4c "A" Sub Light ECHELON. 2Lieut. R.C. NORTON posted from Base & attached "B" Sub. Light Echelon.	

CAPT. R.F.A.
OMMDG. 2nd CAV. DIV. AMN COLUMN.

CONFIDENTIAL.

WAR DIARY

of

2nd CAVALRY DIVISIONAL AMMUNITION COLUMN.

DECEMBER, 1916.

VOL. XXVIII.

Army Form C. 2118.

WAR DIARY
2nd Cavalry Divn⁰ Ammunition Column R.H.A.
INTELLIGENCE SUMMARY.

(Erase heading not required.)

Instructions regarding War Diaries and Intelligence Summaries are contained in F. S. Regs., Part II. and the Staff Manual respectively. Title pages will be prepared in manuscript.

Hour, Date, Place	Summary of Events and Information	Remarks and references to Appendices
1.12.16 to 31.12.16. ESTREES-les-CRECY.	Remained in billets at ESTREES-les-CRECY. As many wagons as could be spared were sent daily to assist the farmers in carrying the sugar beet from the collecting dépôt at LIGESCOURT to the sugar factory at CRÉCY.	

R. J. Grunn
Col R.F.A.
Commanding 2nd Cavalry Division Amm: Col:
R.H.A.

CONFIDENTIAL.

WAR   DIARY

of

2nd CAVALRY DIVISIONAL AMMUNITION COLUMN.

JANUARY, 1917.

VOL. XXIX.

Army Form C. 2118.

WAR DIARY
2nd Cavalry Division or Ammunition Column R.F.A.
INTELLIGENCE SUMMARY.
(Erase heading not required.)

SR/257

Instructions regarding War Diaries and Intelligence Summaries are contained in F.S. Regs., Part II. and the Staff Manual respectively. Title pages will be prepared in manuscript.

Hour, Date, Place	Summary of Events and Information	Remarks and references to Appendices
9.1.14 ESTREES-les-CRECY	2/Lieut W. LUCAS, R.F.A. admitted to Hospital	
9.1.14 "	Capt C.C. THICKNESSE (C of E Chaplain) temporarily attached.	
26.1.14 "	2/Lieut G. DANIA R.F.A. to 34th Divisional Artillery. Ammunition was given to local inhabitants for covering sugar beet and in spreading manure on the land during the month.	
17.1.17 "	2/Lieut W. LUCAS R.F.A. evacuated to ENGLAND.	

R. Train Capt R.F.A.
Commdg 2nd Cav. Div. Am. Column.

CONFIDENTIAL.

Vol 26

WAR DIARY

of

2nd CAVALRY DIVISIONAL AMMUNITION COLUMN.

FEBRUARY, 1917.
VOL. XXX.
==============

Army Form C. 2118.

WAR DIARY
INTELLIGENCE SUMMARY.

(Erase heading not required.) 2nd Cavalry Division Amm. Col. R.H.A.

Instructions regarding War Diaries and Intelligence Summaries are contained in F. S. Regs., Part II. and the Staff Manual respectively. Title pages will be prepared in manuscript.

Hour, Date, Place	Summary of Events and Information	Remarks and references to Appendices
4.2.17 ESTREES-les-CRECY	3Lieut A.H. JEFFREYS R.F.A. joined from 11th DIVISIONAL ARTILLERY.	
5.2.17 - do -	2Lieut K.C. HADOW R.F.A. joined from 12th DIVISIONAL ARTILLERY	
12.2.17 - do -	2Lieut A.H. JEFFREYS R.F.A. posted to "D" BATTERY R.H.A.	
16.2.17 - do -	2Lieut K.C. HADOW R.F.A. posted to "D" BATTERY, R.H.A.	
	The month was spent in re-drilling the NCOs & awaiting the local trainers.	

John W. Ayd
Capt 2nd Cav Div Amm Col
R.H.A.

CONFIDENTIAL.

WAR   DIARY

of

2nd CAVALRY DIVISIONAL AMMUNITION COLUMN.

MARCH, 1917.

VOL. XXXI.

WAR DIARY
INTELLIGENCE SUMMARY
(Erase heading not required.)

Army Form C. 2118.

Hour, Date, Place	Summary of Events and Information	Remarks and references to Appendices
1.3.17 Estrees les Crecy	Tempy Captain H.F. TRIM admitted to Hospital.	
9.3.17	Tempy Captain H.F. TRIM struck off strength.	
15.3.17	Lieut C.H. BORTHWICK joined from Y By R.H.A.	
21.3.17	Capt J. PERRY joined from 6th D.A.C. R.F.A.	
23.3.17	2Lieut R.H. BAILEY joined from Base.	
	The Column remained in billets during the whole month. A certain amount of help was given the bread inhabitants.	

J Perry. Capt R.F.A.
Commdg. 2nd Cav. Div. Am. Col. E.A.H.A.

CONFIDENTIAL.

WAR DIARY

of

2nd CAVALRY DIVISIONAL AMMUNITION COLUMN.

APRIL, 1917.

VOL. XXXII.

WAR DIARY
or
INTELLIGENCE SUMMARY.

(Erase heading not required.)

2nd Cavalry Division Ammn. Col R.H.A.

Instructions regarding War Diaries and Intelligence Summaries are contained in F.S. Regs., Part II. and the Staff Manual respectively. Title pages will be prepared in manuscript.

Army Form C. 2118.

Hour, Date, Place	Summary of Events and Information	Remarks and references to Appendices
10 AM. 5.4.17 ESTREES LES CRECY to 4 PM 5.4.17 BEALCOURT	The Heavy and Small Arms Echelon marched from ESTREES-LES-CRECY to BEALCOURT.	
2 PM 8.4.17 BEALCOURT to 10 PM 8.4.17 HENU	The Column marched to HENU. A, B and C Subsections attached to J, F and D Batteries "Light Echelon" respectively joined the Heavy Echelon on the line of march and marched to new billets at HENU.	
9.4.17. HENU	The Subsections of the Light Echelon rejoined the Batteries & accompanied them into action.	
12. MIDN.10.4.17 HENU	9 limbered G.S. Wagons in charge of 2Lt J.W.AIRD R.F.A. proceeded to ARRAS. to supply the Country with ammunition if required.	
11.4.17 HENU.	The 9 limbered G.S. Wagons above rejoined the Heavy Echelon at HENU.	
12.4.17 HENU.	The Subsections of the Light Echelon rejoined the Heavy Echelon at HENU.	

P.T.O.

Army Form C. 2118.

WAR DIARY
or
INTELLIGENCE SUMMARY.

(Erase heading not required.) Divisional Artillery 2nd Cavalry Col RHA

Hour, Date, Place	Summary of Events and Information	Remarks and references to Appendices
	Continued	
9 AM. 20.4.17. HENU.	B detraction Light Echelon in charge of Lt R.C. NORTON was re-attached to E Battery R.H.A. and accompanied the Battery to new billets.	
9 AM 24.4.17 HENU.	C detraction Light Echelon in charge of 2Lt C.J.E ROBINSON T.F.A. was re-attached to "D" Battery R.H.A.	
27.4.17 HENU.	2Lt R.H BAILEY R.F.A was posted to 50TH Divisional Artillery for duty.	
30.4.17. HENU.	The Heavy Echelon remains at HENU.	

J. Perry Capt RHA
Commdg 2nd Cav. Div. Am. Column, R.H.A.

CONFIDENTIAL.

WAR DIARY

of

2nd CAV. DIVL. AMMUNITION COLUMN. R.H.A.

MAY, 1917 — VOL. XXXIII.

Army Form C. 2118.

WAR DIARY
or
INTELLIGENCE SUMMARY.

(Erase heading not required.) Ammunition Column 2nd Cavalry Division

Instructions regarding War Diaries and Intelligence Summaries are contained in F.S. Regs., Part II. and the Staff Manual respectively. Title pages will be prepared in manuscript.

Hour, Date, Place	Summary of Events and Information	Remarks and references to Appendices
9 AM 12.5.17. HENU –	The Column marched from HENU to NAOURS.	
5 PM 12.5.17. NAOURS		
7 AM 13.5.17. NAOURS - AUBIGNY	The Column marched from NAOURS to AUBIGNY arriving at 4 PM	
13.5.17 AUBIGNY	2Lt G.P. HEDGES RFA joined from Base.	
9 AM 14.5.17. AUBIGNY - LAMOTTE	The Column marched from AUBIGNY to LAMOTTE.	
14.5.17 AUBIGNY	2Lt M.N. DEWING. RFA posted to 3rd Divisional Artillery	
7 AM 15.5.17 LAMOTTE - MARQUAIX	The Column from LAMOTTE to MARQUAIX and encamped in the open at a point about 1000 yards N.E. of the village.	
16.5.17. MARQUAIX	2Lt J.W. AIRD. RFA was sent to take charge of an Ammunition Refilling Point situated on the road RONSEL-St EMILIE.	
19.5.17 – do –	2Lt G.P HEDGES RFA attached to 'E' Battery RHA	
19.5.17 – do –	'A' subsection Light Echelon AC &c of 1st CH BORTHWICK RFA was reattached to 'J' Battery RHA	
31.5.17 – do –	The Column remains in camp at MARQUAIX.	

.... Capt. R.F.A.
Comm'd'g 2nd Cav Div. Am'n Column, B.H.A.

CONFIDENTIAL

War Diary
of
2nd Cavalry Division Ammunition Column

from 1st June to 30th June 1917.

Volume XXXIV

WAR DIARY or INTELLIGENCE SUMMARY

(Erase heading not required.) R.H.A. 2nd Cavalry Division

Ammunition Column

Instructions regarding War Diaries and Intelligence Summaries are contained in F.S. Regs., Part II. and the Staff Manual respectively. Title pages will be prepared in manuscript.

Army Form C. 2118.

Hour, Date, Place	Summary of Events and Information	Remarks and references to Appendices
MARQUAIX 2.6.17	Capt J Andrew A.V.C. joined from Base and took over duties of Veterinary Officer to Div. Shnt.;	
— do — 14.6.17	2 Lt J.W Aird R.F.A rejoined from A.R.P.	
MARQUAIX 1.6.17 to 30.6.17	The Column remained in camp at MARQUAIX during the whole month. Two parties, one of 24 men and 32 horses and one of 18 men and 24 horses, have been engaged in Haymaking and Agricultural Corps and Divisional area. in Haymaking and Agricultural work. These parties form part of the Agricultural Establishment of the 2nd Cavalry Division. N.B. Horses have been grazed daily, and much improvement in condition can be noted since the Column arrived in present area.	

J. Purr .... Capt. R.F.A.
Comm. 2nd Cav. Div. Amm. Column, R.H.A.

CONFIDENTIAL

WAR DIARY
of
AMMUNITION COLUMN R.H.A
2ND CAVALRY DIVISION

from 1st to 31st July 1917

Volume No XXXV

WAR DIARY
or
INTELLIGENCE SUMMARY

(Erase heading not required.) Ammunition Column RHA 2nd Cavalry Division

Hour, Date, Place	Summary of Events and Information	Remarks and references to Appendices
7.7.17. MARQUAIX	2/Lt C.J.F. ROBINSON. R.F.A. posted to "D" Battery R.H.A.	R
11.7.17. MARQUAIX	2/Lt R.A. TOWNSHEND. R.F.A. posted from "D" Battery R.H.A. (Remaining with "D" Battery R.H.A. as "C" Sub. light Echelon.)	R
13.7.17. " — SUZANNE	2/Lt J.H. MASSEY. R.F.A. joined from 15th Divnl Artillery. (attached for duty.) The Column marched to SUZANNE arriving in camp at 3.30 P.M.	R R
6.AM 14.7.17. SUZANNE — VILLE SOR CORBIE.	The Column marched to VILLE SOR CORBIE arriving at 9.30 A.M.	R
6.A.M. 15.7.17. VILLE SOR CORBIE — SARTON	Marched to SARTON. arriving at 10.30 A.M.	R
6.AM 16.7.17. SARTON — LUCHEUX	Marched to LUCHEUX arriving at 9.40.A.M.	R
12 NOON 27.7.17. LUCHEUX — LA THIELOYE.	The 13 Pdr. section of the Ammn Column (consisting of 2/O.Z.S. Wagons), marched with the Brigade to LA THIELOYE, and was placed under the orders of First Army.	R
LUCHEUX.	The S.A.A. section remained at LUCHEUX, under the command of 2/Lt J.W. AIRD. R.F.A.	

P.T.O

WAR DIARY
INTELLIGENCE SUMMARY

(Erase heading not required.) RHA 2nd Cavalry Division Ammunition Column

Hour, Date, Place	Summary of Events and Information	Remarks and references to Appendices
11.30 AM 28.7.17 LA THIEUGE – OLHAIN	The 13 Pdr Section marched to OLHAIN arriving at 3.25 p.m.	JR
9.30 AM. 29.7.17 OLHAIN – SAILLY-LABOURSE	The 13 Pdr Section marched to SAILLY-LABOURSE arriving at 1.15 P.M.	JR
29.7.17 LUCHEUX – BERLENCOURT	The S.A.A. Section marched to BERLENCOURT.	JR
31.7.17 SAILLY – LABOURSE	The 13 Pdr. Section remains in camp at SAILLY-LABOURSE.	JR

Capt. R.F.A.
Commdg. 2nd Cav. Div. Amn. Colne, R.H.A.

Vol 32

CONFIDENTIAL

War Diary of the Ammunition Column RHA 2nd Cavalry Division

from 1.8.17 to 31.8.17

VOLUME XXXVII

CONFIDENTIAL

Army Form C. 2118.

WAR DIARY
or
INTELLIGENCE SUMMARY

(Erase heading not required.) Ammunition Column 2nd Cavalry Division R.H.A

Instructions regarding War Diaries and Intelligence Summaries are contained in F.S. Regs., Part II. and the Staff Manual respectively. Title pages will be prepared in manuscript.

Hour, Date, Place	Summary of Events and Information	Remarks and references to Appendices
1.8.17. to 19.8.17. SAILLY LABOURSE	The 13 Pdr Section of the Ammn Col. was attached to 6th Divnl Artillery whilst the Brigade was in action.	
2.8.17. BERLENCOURT	Lt J.N.H. WILSON. RHA joined the SAA Section on posting from 1st Cavalry Division	
4.8.17 — " —	Lt J.N.H. WILSON RHA proceeded to take charge of the Light Echelon intructor attached to "D" Battery RHA	
9.8.17. — " —	2Lt K.A. TOWNSHEND RFA. joined SAA Section at BERLENCOURT from attached to "D" Battery RHA.	
19.8.17. SAILLY LABOURSE — CHATEAU OLHAIN —	The 13 Pdr Section marched from SAILLY LABOURSE to CHATEAU HOUDAIN upon receipt of orders to rejoin 2nd Cavalry Division	
20.8.17. CHATEAU OLHAIN — BERLENCOURT	13 Pdr Section marched from HOUDAIN to BERLENCOURT and rejoined SAA Section.	
31.8.17 BERLENCOURT.	The Column remains in camp at BERLENCOURT.	

Capt. R.F.A.
Commdg. 2nd Cav. Div. Amn. Column, R.H.A.

CONFIDENTIAL

No. 3

WAR DIARY

of

AMMUNITION COLUMN RHA
2nd CAVALRY DIVISION

from SEPT 1st to 30th 1917

VOLUME XXXVII

Army Form C. 2118.

WAR DIARY
or
INTELLIGENCE SUMMARY. (Erase heading not required.)

Ammunition Column . R.H.A. 2nd Cavalry Division

VOLUME XXXVIII

Instructions regarding War Diaries and Intelligence Summaries are contained in F.S. Regs., Part II. and the Staff Manual respectively. Title pages will be prepared in manuscript.

Hour, Date, Place		Summary of Events and Information	Remarks and references to Appendices
6.30 AM	5.9.17 BERLENCOURT – BAJUS	The 13 Pdr. Section of the Column came under the orders of the 1st Army and marched with the Brigade to BAJUS, arriving at 3 P.M.	J.P.
9.0 AM	5.9.17	The SAA Section marched to new billets at FLERS	J.P.
	6.9.17 BAJUS – HESDINGUEL	The 13 Pdr. Section marched to HESDINGUEL arriving at 12.30 P.M.	J.P.
	8.9.17 HESDINGUEL – FOSSE No 2 (2000 yds W of LES BREBIS)	The 13 Pdr. Section marched, and arrived in camp situated behind Fosse No 2. 2000 yds west of LES BREBIS at 11.40 A.M.	J.P.
15.9.17	FOSSE No 2 – VERQUINEL	The 13 Pdr. Section marched to VERQUINEL	J.P.
16.9.17	FLERS.	2LT. J.W. AIRD RFA left the SAA Section on posting to 38th Division	J.P.
21.9.17	VERQUINEL – BETHUNE	The 13 Pdr. Section marched to BETHUNE and billeted in the Tobacco Factory	J.P.
25.9.17	BETHUNE	2LT. B.B. EDGE RFA joined from the Base.	J.P.
25.9.17	FLERS	2LT W MURE RFA joined the SAA Section at FLERS from the Base.	J.P.
30.9.17	FLERS.	The SAA Section remained at FLERS. During the month, a great deal of help has been given to the French inhabitants with our 9 horses in assisting in gathering the harvest	J.P.
30.9.17	BETHUNE	The 13 Pdr. Section remained with the Brigade, attached to the 6th Divisional Artillery	J.P.

Cent
Capt. R.F.A.
Commdg. 2nd Cav. Div. Amn. Column, R.H.A.

Vol 34

CONFIDENTIAL

WAR DIARY of the
AMMUNITION COLUMN
R H A
2nd Cavalry Division
from 1st October to 31st October 1917

VOLUME XXXVIII

Army Form C. 2118.

WAR DIARY
or
INTELLIGENCE SUMMARY.
(Erase heading not required.)

Ammunition Column RHA 2nd Cavalry Divison

Hour, Date, Place	Summary of Events and Information	Remarks and references to Appendices
1.10.17	Lt R C NORTON posted to F Battery RHA	Nil
8.10.17 FLERS – LA THIEULOYE	The EAA section marched from FLERS to LA THIEULOYE under orders of 2nd Cavalry Divison	Nil
9 AM 9.10.17 BETHUNE – LA THIEULOYE	The 13 Pdr Section marched from BETHUNE and joined AAC Section at LA THIEULOYE	Nil
12.10.17 LA THIEULOYE	2/Lt B.B. EDGE RFA posted to J Battery RHA	Nil
9.30AM 20.10.17 LA THIEULOYE – ETREE WAMIN	The Column marched under orders of the 2nd Cavalry Brigade from LA THIEULOYE to ETREE WAMIN en route for AMIENS area	Nil
9.30AM 21.10.17 ETREE WAMIN – ST LEGER.DOMART	March was continued from ETREE WAMIN to ST LEGER-AES-DOMART.	Nil
9.15AM 22.10.17 ST LEGER-lès-DOMART – PLACHY-BUYON	The Column marched from ST LEGER lès DOMART and arrived in bivouac area at PLACHY-BUYON.	Nil
31.10.17 PLACHY-BUYON	The Column remains in billets and the training of men and horses is in an indication with regard to Horsemanship of NCOs and men is the primary [signature]	Nil

Commdg. 2nd Cav. Div. Amn. Column, R.H.A.

CONFIDENTIAL

WAR DIARY of
AMMUNITION COLUMN RHA
      2nd Cavalry Division
   1st to 30th NOVEMBER 1917

VOLUME I

Army Form C. 2118.

WAR DIARY
or
INTELLIGENCE SUMMARY.
(Erase heading not required.)

Ammunition Column R.H.A. 2nd Cavalry Division

Hour, Date, Place	Summary of Events and Information	Remarks and references to Appendices
12 Noon 16.11.17 Plachy-Buyon – Proyart	The Column marched to Proyart in accordance with orders from 2nd Cav. Div. arriving at 10.15 P.M.	JL
4 P.M. 17.11.17 Proyart – Montecourt	The march was continued to Montecourt (Monchy-Lagache) the Column arriving in new camp at 12 midnight 17-18.11.17	JL
2 A.M. 21.11.17 Montecourt – Villers-Faucon	During the night of the 20th/21st inst. the Column moved to Villers-Faucon arriving in camp at 9 A.M.	JL
9 P.M. 21.11.17 Villers-Faucon – Villers-Plouich	The S.A.A. (light section) consisting of 9 R.S.J. Wagons moved forward with 'A' Echelon of the Division in readiness to supply Cavalry Regts if required. The remainder of the Column were held in readiness to move from Villers-Faucon to the forward area if required.	JL
10 A.M. 22.11.17 — " —	The R.G.S. Wagons returned to Villers-Faucon from Villers-Plouich.	JL
6 P.M. 23.11.17 Villers-Faucon	The L.G.S. Wagons again moved forward with 'A' Echelon and remained with same until 30.11.17	JL
7/30 A.M. 30.11.17 Villers-Faucon	preparatory to moving from the Villers-Faucon area. The L.G.S. Wagons were recalled by an urgent message & reported 'A' Echelon at 2nd Cav. Div. accordingly.	JL
12 Noon 30.11.17 Villers-Faucon		JL

J Scott
Comdg. 2nd Cav. Div. Am. Column, R.H.A.

CONFIDENTIAL

War Diary of the
Ammunition Column RHA
2nd Cavalry Division
from 1st to 31st December 1917
VOLUME XL

WAR DIARY
OR
INTELLIGENCE SUMMARY.

(Erase heading not required.)

Ammunition Column R.H.A. 2nd Cavalry Division

Hour, Date, Place		Summary of Events and Information	Remarks and references to Appendices
6 P.M. 1.12.17	VILLERS-FAUCON - FINS	The Column marched to a point 1000 yards N. of FINS and camped	
10 A.M. 2.12.17	FINS - ETRICOURT	The Column marched to ETRICOURT	
3 P.M. 2.12.17	ETRICOURT	The 9 LGS wagons (which had been recalled to "A" Echelon of the 2nd Cav. Divn on the night of 30-11-17) regained.	
11 A.M. 6.12.17	ETRICOURT - METZ	The 13 Pdr section marched to 1 kilometre N. of METZ-en-COUTRE	
11 A.M. 6.12.17	ETRICOURT - SUZANNE	The SAA section of 1st KRA Townsend RFA marched with "B" Echelon of the 2nd Cav Divn to SUZANNE en route for the AMIENS area.	
7.12.17	SUZANNE - VERS	The SAA section arrived in billeting area and billeted at VERS	
8.12.17	METZ - BOUCLY	The 13 Pdr section marched with the 3rd Bde RHA to BOUCLY	
12.12.17	BOUCLY	Lt. C.H. BORTHWICK (attached to "J" Battery RHA of of Reght Echelon) was admitted to Hospital	
14.12.17	BOUCLY	2Lt. W. MURE RFA was posted to "J" Battery RHA for duty.	
31.12.17	BOUCLY	The 13 Pdr section remains with the Remnds at BOUCLY	
31.12.17	VERS	The SAA section remains with the 2nd Cavalry Division at VERS	

J. Pim Capt. R.H.A.
Commdg. 2nd Cav. Divn Amm. Column, R.H.A.

CONFIDENTIAL

WAR DIARY

of

AMMUNITION COLUMN, 3rd BRIGADE. R.H.A.

1st January 1918 to 31st January 1918

VOLUME XLI

WAR DIARY
or
INTELLIGENCE SUMMARY.

Army Form C. 2118.

Place	Date	Hour	Summary of Events and Information	Remarks and references to Appendices
BOUCLY	8.1.18	11 AM	The 13th Sch. Section marched to CAULAINCOURT.	
CAULAINCOURT	24.1.18		2/Lt R.K.A. KENNEDY R.F.A. (S.R.) joined the Column from "A" Battery 84th Army Brigade R.F.A. for duty with the Light Echelon attached to "J" Battery R.H.A.	
			Since arrival at CAULAINCOURT a Watering party & Ammunition Dump fatigue have been detailed & arms have been issued to our R.E. Surveying medical etc	

..........J Curry........ Capt. R.F.A.
Commanding 2nd Cav. Div. Amm. Column. R.F.A.

CONFIDENTIAL

WAR DIARY
OF
AMMUNITION COLUMN 3rd BRIGADE. R.H.A

FROM FEBRUARY 1st to 28th. 1918

VOLUME XLIII

Army Form C. 2118.

WAR DIARY
or
INTELLIGENCE SUMMARY.
(Erase heading not required.)

Feby 1918

Place	Date	Hour	Summary of Events and Information	Remarks and references to Appendices
CAULAINCOURT	1/2/18 to 28.2.18		The Ammunition Column is still in bivouac in CAULAINCOURT. During the month working parties were found to build new Ammunition dumps near VERMAND - and teams were used for carting R.E. material, also considerable amount of hut implements have been made.	J. H. W.
"	12/2/18		2/Lt R HAWKES joined the Unit from the BASE.	J.H.W.
"	20/2/18		Capt J. Perry R.H.A. (O.C. Ammn Column 3rd Brigade R.H.A.) proceeded on leave to United Kingdom	J.H.W.
"	20/2/18		Lt (a/A) H. WILKES. Head Quarters 3rd Brigade R.H.A. took over temporary command of the Ammunition Column during the absence, on leave, of Captain J. PERRY.	J.H.W.
"	26/2/18		2/Lt R.J. HAWKES admitted to hospital.	W.H.W.

Th. H. Wilkes Lt. R.F.A.
Commdg. 2nd Cav. Div. Ammn. Column, R.H.A.

www.ingramcontent.com/pod-product-compliance
Lightning Source LLC
Chambersburg PA
CBHW081555160426

43191CB00011B/1935